# *Yielding*

The 'Becoming' Years

*The third account in the inspirational*
**Relinquish & Reap Series**

*Jessica Janna*

&

*April Alisa Marquette*

*Dear Reader,*

*I wanted you to know that My April and I chose the jasmine flower to grace the cover of this book because it is beautiful. As flower lovers, we also chose jasmine because it can be a shrub or a vine. It grows and climbs, and reminds me of my journey — the human journey. Jasmine flowers belong to the olive family and are pleasantly fragrant. The petals are unbelievably soft, but...they only last for a season. Human life is similar; the softness and the fragrance do not last forever. However, the memories can linger a lifetime.*

*In life, many changes and hurdles are encountered. Yet we should never forget that every experience can aid us to do one of a few things. We can learn, grow, get something, or give something.*

*With this purse-sized book, I would like to remind you that life will never be all one thing. It will never be all bad; neither will it be all good. It is a curious mix of things, and this mix can enable us to better ourselves and even others. Most assuredly, life allows us to garner precious knowledge from every one of our experiences, both pleasant and not.*

*Today, I urge you to look anew at the jasmine flower. Then I suggest you think of yourself. Like jasmine, you too can leave a lovely lingering fragrance. It doesn't matter where you go or with whom you interact; you can leave a precious portion of your essence. If you haven't done so in the past, start this day. Allow the Holy Spirit to guide and temper you —let Him guide your words as well as your actions. When you feel a little nudge telling you to be quiet, do so. If you feel a nudge to offer someone comfort, do so. As you follow these urgings, the Holy Spirit will become more assertive in your life. After eighty-some years, I should know.*

*Then like the jasmine flower, memories of you will be sweet. Like the vine, you too will reach and climb. You may even attain things that you never thought you could. Remember, yours is a life of purpose. Yours is, and can further be, a life of reaping. This only happens when we relinquish. Don't dwell on the bad. Don't allow hurtful things to consume you. My daughter says, "Don't let them take up mental real estate." Do as the Bible says in Philippians the 4th chapter and the 8th verse:*

'…Whatsoever things are true, whatsoever things are honest, whatsoever things are just, whatsoever things are pure, whatsoever things are lovely, whatsoever things are of good report; if there be any virtue, and if there be any praise, think on these things.' KJV

*Allow the untoward situations that have, and will, arise in your life to make you stronger. Let them create wisdom; let them make you more loving. Allow circumstances to make you better, not bitter.*

*My dear, never forget to let go and let God…*

*Relinquish and reap,*

*Jessie*

Thou wilt show me the path of life: in thy presence is fullness of joy; at thy right hand there are pleasures for evermore. *KJV*

*Psalms 16:11*

Table of Contents

Table of Contents
*Continued*

## *Inspiration and a Prayer*

I was going to New York! It was a dream come true. When I first heard there was a possibility that I could go, I had no idea how the Holy Spirit would make it a reality. However, later, I was on a train with beautiful teachers from the High School. Then all I could think about was the ad that had publicized job openings for day work—in New York. I was going to work in *New York*!

I guess the teachers were excited too. Previously, they'd said that to make money over the summer, they wanted to do something besides teaching. I kept remembering that some of them had watched me sing in school, some of them had attended my family church. They'd watched me grow up, and now they and I –we—were off!

Like the mover and shaker that my mother had been, I'd gotten in the wind. I'd said my prayers, often, because I'd been aware that I had to leave Arkansas, for the second time. Then I knew I'd been inspired to move to New York. I'll never let anyone tell me that the Holy Spirit was not leading me.

At the time, I knew I would not know a soul in that city, no one other than the young lady teachers with whom I was traveling. Still, upon hearing about rich people who were hiring help, I knew the way was being paved for me, a tall, slender, brown young woman, so that in my life, I might make a much-needed change.

Just to refresh your memory, or give others a little background; in the second book of this series, *Sowing*, I believe I mentioned that when some people back at Trinity, the family church, found out my plans, they told me that I would not make it 'up north.' Isn't that what certain people do? They'll strangle your hopes and dreams—if you let them. Maybe those people meant well. Perhaps they simply believed I should stay where I was seemingly building a life. Or maybe those people wanted out and were jealous that it looked like I was getting out. I knew of others who felt hurt; out loud, they wondered why? They asked why I wanted to leave. They wanted to know what was so bad about staying in Arkansas.

The truth is I didn't so much *want* to leave. I was being pulled away. I felt I was being called, by the Holy Spirit. In my first book, *Seedling*, which details my youngest years, I told you that I always knew I would leave the state where I'd been as a child. I always felt the need to; for me, things never seemed exactly right. I never really fit. At the time, I had no idea that to be called away was the chosen path for my life. I simply knew I felt the urge to go, to move. I wanted a different type of life. Thus, I knew I was being led to go to New York.

Back when I'd been a youngling, I'd prayed. I'd asked the Holy Spirit if going away was indeed for me; I said if it was, please provide a way. I had no money to speak of, and I knew no one in the big city. I had no connections, and as far as I knew, at the time, there might not have been a job waiting for me. Yet I had to make that journey, *if* the Holy Spirit made it possible. And that is just what He did! I knew it when I heard of job openings for day work.

A few teachers, young women who also desired to do and experience something different, heeded the call, too. Some of the teachers I knew from when I'd been a growing girl. Two of them were the Berry Sisters. They were very attractive, with the loveliest personalities. One, whom I'll call Bee, was short with a beautiful, round face. Her hair was prettily arranged, and she was a little lighter in complexion than me. Her sister had a bubbly winning personality. The sister was considered more the hang-out one, the fun one. She had very long hair. Sister, the fun one was plump-ish too, with a nice figure. Both of them, and I, looked at this going away sort of like it would be a summer adventure.

However, I didn't just have the summer on my mind. I'd already decided; I was simply going to follow the leading of the Holy Spirit. I was going to see where I would wind up—for however long. I won't say I wasn't nervous because I was, but I had the Lord on my side.

Going to New York proved to be quite a ride. Along the way, those extraordinary ladies and I shared laughter and conversation. Aloud, we wondered what we would find at our journey's end. I believe I was even excited. I know I wondered what kind of work we would do. However, I didn't think about living in the city or near the Statue of Liberty. I simply tried to settle my insides, since I'd made up my mind that I was going. I even said to myself more than once, "I am not going back to Arkansas. I am going to stay and find work and…whatever."

I knew that I might feel scared and alone at times because I was, in essence, journeying alone. I knew too that I had felt those things at different times in my life. Still, I remembered that there had been God all throughout. The wisdom of His Holy Spirit had moved me out of many harmful situations. He had done so simply because I'd never relinquished my faith in Him, no matter what happened. I'd sought the Holy Spirit again and again, and His presence had carried me. Sure, I was young, in my early twenties, but I knew He would continue to do so, even on this leg of my journey.

It seemed to be taking a long time, the ride on that Greyhound bus…but when the teachers and I finally wound up in New York, we were amazed—because what a place! I mean there were so many buildings. The structures were so tall. There was so much to see and hear. There were people, and so many of them, going every which way! Some had pushcarts and were selling things. There was so much noise too. Traffic, like I hadn't seen before, was a colorful snarl, and there was so much going on, all at one time…

# A Whole New World

When the teachers and I first got to New York, there were so many things to see, I could hardly take it all in. To this day, eighty-some years later, I don't remember seeing any landmarks. Everything was just a blur. All I remember are swirls of color, and there was movement. I remember that the teachers and I were picked up by someone in a van. That person drove us to an office in the suburbs. There was where we received our assignments. It was like job corps, where young people go and find out what they will soon do.

I vaguely recall going to the house where I would begin work. It was unlike anything I had ever lived in; the neighborhood, too. Where I'd previously lived had been okay, but back there and here were worlds apart! Here, all was beautiful and so well-tended. The surrounding area was green, with flowers artfully spilling onto pathways. The street was wide, and there were so many other daunting houses with gleaming windows. There were passing cars, but only every once in a while.

At that residence, I became acquainted with the people for whom I would work. They spoke in measured, level voices. They reiterated what would be expected of me, and I dutifully took it all in.

In the same township, I found out that the teachers were stationed not far from me. One was in Woodmere, and she and I could walk to meet each other. Of that, I was glad as I digested what would be expected of me. I was told there would be a little light cooking—you know, making lunch for the children of whom I would take care. I would need to keep those children clean, I'd been told; I was to make sure they didn't hurt themselves when they got rowdy, as they would. It was my job to keep a close eye on them, especially when we were outside. When we were inside, they couldn't just go tearing up things, either. They needed supervision.

As the days passed, I did all that was required and more. I would play games with the children. In the mornings, I'd get them ready for school. Evenings, after homework at a specific time, I would be off-duty. I could not complain since I was not there to be a maid—this family had one. I felt the work was okay. I thought it was something I could do. I had, after all, looked after Baby Brother when he'd been but a little thing, and I had done an excellent job of it, I must say.

Although I worked for wealthy people, some of my traveling mates got families that weren't as well off. Like me, some of them got nice people, while unfortunately, a few of the teachers wound up with not-so-nice people. Yet it wasn't something that they couldn't deal with. As you know, we'd all set out on this journey to explore, to inject a little adventure into our lives, and change the humdrum every day to something meaningful. So this was it.

As I settled in, I realized that before I'd journeyed to New York, I'd wanted to change my life. I'd always been on a quest for better. I realized that I hadn't wanted to just be a dreamer all along. I wanted to be a person whose dreams come true. Manifestation is what you hear a lot about today.

Back then, there I was, in a place where I was learning things of which I had never dreamed. My employers often mentioned something to me in passing. These were things that expanded my mental horizons. I was glad for the knowledge.

That summer, the teachers and I had our own rooms on those jobs, and I even had a small bathroom to myself, maybe because I was black. The teachers and I were free to do as we wished on weekends, so we explored the adjacent towns and the city. On our first weekend off, I had been allowed to use the house phone to arrange to meet my friends. Later, we met up with each other.

We met in Hewlett and went looking for churches. In time, we learned how to get around on mass transportation. Within my new city, I got pretty good at navigating. But that first weekend, a cab driver suggested some churches and where they were located. That was why on Sundays, the teachers and I found ourselves in church. We met at the Long Island Rail Road, and we were off! We went to a church called Gethsemane, where Elder Burroughs was the pastor. We went to a church on Redfern Avenue too, then pastored by Elder Kelly. At both churches, I felt comfortable. The people, all of whom looked like me, were welcoming and the services touched something deep within me.

By now, you are aware that the teachers with whom I had journeyed knew me in and out of school. They knew my background and vocal excellence. Thus they were supportive of the gifts and talents that they had seen in me. Most wished me well. Determined to push me further, one Sunday as we sat in a worship service, unbeknownst to me, one of the ladies wrote out a note.

The church's music leader and the pastor saw that this teacher's note requested that I be allowed to sing.

Unaware of this, imagine my surprise at hearing my name called. I learned, along with the other congregants, that I would sing a solo. That was when I heard my mother's voice, inside, telling me what she had when I'd been a growing girl. *Do your best.*

Well, I did what I'd always done. I stepped to the podium and gave it my all. When I began to sing *In Times like these, we need a savior/ we need an anchor*, I wound up in a zone where my voice became not my own, but an instrument through which the Holy Spirit could minister to those who listened. It was—and is—a mystical state, one of great passion, release, and surrender. It is a transcendent state, one acknowledged by many traditions that have monastic histories…Buddhism, Hinduism, and Christianity, to name a few.

When I finished, there weren't many dry eyes in the place.

Afterward, I was asked to sing on another upcoming occasion. That became the first of an outpouring of the same type of invitations.

## *Nice Work If You Can Get It*

Although the teachers and I visited different churches, I spent the summer searching for the place of worship that would become my very own. The teachers and I met on weekends, often in Far Rockaway. Some of those for whom we worked let us use their phones. The majority were decent people who lived in fantastic houses. There, I learned etiquette—the code of acceptable social behavior. I learned about floral arranging, and how to set a fabulous table. I learned about Kosher and non-Kosher and how this pertained to people of Jewish descent.

Oh, I learned many things that wound up serving me well throughout my life. However, sometimes a job didn't last very long. Maybe the children got older and wound up going to school all day, or things didn't work out; then I'd wind up with a different position. These came in the years to follow. Sometimes I wound up with a white family where I would have to do a little day work. You know, some cleaning.

I'll never forget the doctor and his family who lived in Woodmere. They were lovely to me. Then there was a female employer. She might have been in Hewlett; it was so long ago until my memory is a bit foggy on the details. I do know that most were sleep-in jobs. I did basic things like the kid's laundry, ironing, etc. However, the kid's Nanny went to ball games and the beach with them. I still remember something that the lady of the house said to me. All these years later, it has stayed with me.

My employer whispered, "Jessie, if you were an airhead, I wouldn't tell you this…but you have too much going for you to stay in this line of work."

That woman told me I was destined for more, and I believed her. She said she would never say to an airhead the things that she was telling me. She said she could see I had so much to offer. That employer knew about my music. She encouraged me to do pursue it. "Go back to school," was her advice.

I later wound up working for a couple who often fought. I suppose that was just their way. The family was nice enough, though. They had two boys who were about twelve and thirteen. The boys went to school and kept up their rooms. I made salads and lunches for them. I did light washing too, to keep their clothes clean. I folded their clothes and ironed them. However, my employer and his wife, the mother, and the father, were always yelling. I have long since realized. It was their mode of communication.

One day the wife noticed me. I must have looked ill. Then the wife told her husband that they had to cool it, that I didn't like yelling. She said, "We can't fight around Jessie. It gets to her."

The wife was right. I have never been able to abide fighting or bickering. It always ties my stomach in knots, perhaps because I'd had to live through it at a young age, and it had been terrifying.

Another time, I kept a little boy. This boy I often fondly recall. After they came here, I even told my children about him. Regularly, I would tell little Mister to wash his hands. I told that boy that his little white hands had brown dirt on them.

Once, he told me that the palm of my hand was different, and I knew he meant it wasn't pink or white, like his. Anyway, I guess he got tired of me directing him to wash up because there came a day when he cocked his head to the side. Looking at me, without rancor, he announced, "Your *face* is dirty..." Guess he wondered why *I* wasn't washing up, too.

When my daughter became grown, she laughed about this. I know that child said what he did because my face is brown. While hiding a chuckle, I pretended to scold him. I did so by saying, "Get in there and wash yourself." As young as he was, I'm sure he had no idea why I was tickled.

Telling you about that little boy reminds me of a small girl I'd kept while back in Chicago. That girl would sit before the television set watching Popeye the Sailor Man and Olive Oyl. I would have to tell her, several times, to come eat. Once when she ignored me and kept watching TV, I said something, the gist of which was: leave skinny Olive Oyl and come over here. Without turning, Madame Muffie, my little charge, haughtily lisped. I guess she was reprimanding me. Of Olive Oyl, the little girl said, "I shink she's beeyoosheeful."

I also worked for a doctor who would tease me by saying I needed a nice Jewish husband. Dr.

Unger's argument was that "There are plenty of black Jews, you know." Then he would again state, "You need a nice, wealthy, Jewish husband."

I also remember having a room at work. This room was nice, in another fine home in New York. It was on the finished lower level of that home, and that room had its own bathroom. I worked from seven a.m. until dinner, but only on weekdays. After dinner, someone else did the dishes, and I was off-duty until the next day; on that position, until the next day, I no longer had to care for the little ones. Their mother was particular and after hours, she wished to do everything for them.

Everything wasn't roses, though. I worked in places that I didn't like, and for not-great people. I once worked in a place where the kids weren't little.

Once place, the boy was twelve, and his mother had a very nasty disposition. Her face looked like Mardi Gras when she came out without makeup. When I got tired of her foolishness, at the employment agency, I put in for a change.

Due to the type of work I did, I can tell you one thing; whatever your station in life, you can learn something. In life, wherever you are, you can also teach someone else something. From many of those for whom I worked, I learned things. Just because I was a domestic worker did not mean that I did not have pride or dreams of becoming more. Sometimes people who are able to hire others forget that. They think lowly of those who work/care for them. On occasion, I worked for those kinds of people. However, from all of my mother's moving about, I realized. I did not have to stay where someone tried to treat me unkindly. I did not have to be spoken down to or treated as sub-human.

Other employers were the opposite. As a domestic worker, I also experienced being treated well. There were employers who did not treat or see me as lowly. They saw potential in me, and to that, they responded. They pushed me to become better. They even admitted that they had learned things about excellence from me!

So you see, striving to become a better person works both ways. It works from the lowly on up, and from the high on down.

# *Autumn Leaves*

When the summer was over, so was the little 'adventure' for the teachers. The Berry sisters and others had to board the big Greyhound bus headed back to Arkansas. While hugging me, they wondered aloud if I'd be okay. Gently, they suggested that perhaps, I should return home too.

I could not, so I said I'd make it. Sure, I felt a bit discouraged because there I was, facing yet *another* ending. I almost felt like I was being abandoned. I had an actual lump of sadness in my throat. I wanted to cry. I even felt like I'd be a little lost without the teachers, but I had to remind myself; I had always known that just before autumn, those ladies would have to leave. I had tried not to think about it, but they had to go. They had to again pick up the threads of their real lives. I had to remain thankful that they had journeyed as far with me as they had. God had given them to me for a short time. For that, I was grateful because, often, in the past, whenever I had gone anywhere, I had gone alone.

Looking back, I now realize that when the Holy Spirit has a job for one to do, He will allow them to be carried on angel's wings, sometimes. By that, I mean He may give a person others who will be their support—like the Berry sisters were for me, on that first leg of that particular journey. The only thing is… sometimes the support doesn't last, not for long. That's because the Holy Spirit is our only *true* support. This I have learned. God the Father, The Son, and the Holy Spirit; The Holy Trinity, is our Source; of *that* I often remind myself.

Our Source will allow us to meet people and come in contact with personalities that may provide some form of strength to or for us. Our Source will enable these individuals to be in our lives for a time. Sometimes these supporting 'cast members' will even aid us to make our next move, *but* then they will have to go—wherever their lives will take them.

In my case, the Berry sisters and the other teachers had to leave New York, while it was my commission to stay. Therefore, I did what I had always done. I prayed. I worked, and I prayed some more. I knew I was basically alone in the world. I knew I could not make it without my constant companion, the Holy Spirit, so I sang too, and I continued to pray.

Reminded of the little saying about how some people come in our lives and quickly go, and how others may remain for a reason, or a season, I have to tell you. I have learned that faith must not be put in people. We must place it in a higher power, the one *true* Source.

So now I found myself walking, down the streets in Far Rockaway, by myself, again. Just like before. I was a tall, slender, solitary figure, hunched against the wind, making my way, alone. The days were getting shorter and darker, and it was chilly. I needed warmer clothing.

The shift in seasons was beautiful, but for me it was also scary. It was a time of change. With windborne autumn leaves swirling, I was on my way to the church on Redfern Avenue. It sat up high. There, I had met the pastor's daughters who had a younger brother who was twelve or thirteen. With the girls, I'd struck up a friendship. I liked them and vice versa. At their church, I was asked to join the choir.

I went to a district meeting too. There, various churches from that part of New York gathered together to worship. During the worship service, I could often smell the inviting aroma of frying fish or chicken. I knew there would be delicious plates of food sold in the kitchen afterward. Designated people had also baked an assortment of homemade pies or cakes. Slices would be sold, and there would be punch to drink. Many people would get their food, then sit, eat, and fellowship while laughing and chatting. Though I only had money for maybe a slice of pie, I knew. These kinds of meetings, where one can wind up surrounded by other believers, are always a good place to feel as though one genuinely belongs. This is why I often say, *people need a church home.* I've told many people, *you need a church affiliation.* Another reason people need a church home is because everyone can use a physical place to learn the truth of God's word.

At one particular church gathering, I met a very personable young woman. She was dark-skinned, small, and had the most beautiful head of thick hair. You know I always notice hair because I'd been to cosmetology school; back in my second book *Sowing,* I told you about it. Anyway, while most likely standing in the fellowship hall, I found out that this young woman with the thick hair was a member of Gethsemane church.

I'd been to that church before. It was in Inwood, New York. Back in the summer, the teachers and I had attended services there, where Mother and Pop Burroughs were the first lady and pastor. It was to this particular church, that the personable young woman, J, again invited me.

I re-visited Gethsemane. However, then some of my new friends at the other church, where I was friends with the pastor's daughters, became a little peeved. Yes, when they got wind of it.

# *Changes A' Plenty*

As time moved on, I kept going to Gethsemane, which looked like the proverbial little neighborhood church. Outside, there were steps that led up and into a small foyer. Inside, there was a shined wooden floor and a piano in one corner. Mother Burroughs, the first lady, played that piano and sang congregational songs. On the left and the right sides of the sanctuary, the ceiling was sloped. Beneath, on the walls, were windows; I loved that place.

When not in church, I was on my job. However, now, I didn't want to sleep in anymore. Since a good deal of time had passed, a few summers had come and gone; I wanted there to be delineation between my home life and my work life. The only thing was…because I did live-in work, I didn't have a home. I prayed about it, though, because I wanted to make a change.

At church, I would see my new friend with the thick hair. I don't know if I mentioned my desire to J or not, but somehow, the first lady of the church, Mother Burroughs, invited me into her home.

There is a scripture in the bible which is the truth. *Psalms 68* verse *6* says *God sets the solitary in families*. And that is just what He did for me! God caused Mother Burroughs to give me a room, and although I paid rent, she became a mom to me. I will never forget her. She was short and brown, a fine-looking stylish lady with glasses. She had a distinct voice all her own. And Mother Burroughs was so sweet to me. Other times, she instructed me. Her husband was taller than she, slim, with slicked-back hair. They were a dapper couple. Pastor Burroughs was stern. He was a true father figure, and as time passed, I grew to love both of them so much.

Living in their home, I saw that they actually embodied the love of the Lord. They *lived* what they preached. They weren't *on* at Sunday Services and different throughout the week. They were honest and true; and they loved the Lord. They loved His people too. For me, they were undeniable examples of the wisdom and compassion of the Holy Spirit.

Living with Mother and Pastor Burroughs also once again gave me the freedom, and the access, to do what I had when I'd lived in Arkansas. I could again work in the church, with the choir, and teach Sunday school. I was also able to allow the Holy Spirit to use me as I ministered in song.

I have never forgotten that Pastor Burroughs once told the congregation that he called on me to sing because people got healed. He also realized, and said, that the Holy Spirit healed me as I sang.

The Holy Spirit knew that within, I had bewildered and broken places; as do many people.

At the Burroughs' church, I met women I will never forget; Sister Pew and Sister Goodson. One was short, and the other was tall. They were ushers. They wore all white, down to their stockings and gloves. They had shiny pressed 'n curled hair, but more importantly, they had the sweetest spirits.

Those usher ladies always encouraged other young people, and me, to pursue our dreams. There were good deacons too, who did the same. I will forever treasure fond memories of being at Gethsemane church, my home away from home.

I met a young man too, through my personable friend, J. I tell you, her thick hair sometimes shone like pure mink fur. However, back to the young man; to me, it seemed as though many people thought the sun rose and set on him.

He was tall and red. He was what many call a redbone, with reddish undertones in his light brown skin. This young man had sandy brown, close-cut hair, and light-colored eyes. Looking at the way he interacted with others, I could tell. He had been adored by somebody all of his life. He just had that air about him.

Well, it was to this young man that my friend J had bragged. It seems she'd claimed, "Oooh! We got this girl at Gethsemane, and she can sang!" That meant I was pretty good. J said other things; what all, I don't exactly know, but she told it to the tall, adored young man.

I came to find out that in his church district, he was the Minister of Music. Since she'd bragged about me, tall red asked J to bring me to District Choir rehearsal. People said that young man had a good choir. Someone even prompted J to take me to his district meeting, a gathering of churches in Queens, New York.

J and I showed up, and because it was requested, I sang, but I cannot recall the song. Since then, many decades have passed, but I might have sung the hymn, *His Eye Is on the Sparrow.*

After that, J and I found out that the tall red young man's church was on the bus line and that there was a bus that ran right to it. Sometimes we didn't have to take the bus, though; someone would offer us a ride. A bunch of young people would ride or drive from Gethsemane in Inwood to Queens.

That was fun, me, J, and others, getting together and visiting various New York churches, when we didn't have services at our own. It is what young people do, even today. Like we did back then, youngsters go places and sing. They meet others who sometimes become lifelong friends or family. When I did it, God opened doors, enabling me to become known in a place where I had previously known no one, in vast, fast-paced New York.

Later, the tall, adored young man from Queens showed up at Mother Burroughs' house, looking for me. I didn't know what he wanted. I guess I appeared kind of dumb, or puzzled. I can admit it now; I was a bit naïve. From my previous books, you know that my mother kept me close, due to all the happenings. However, it seemed like the red young man, and Mom and Pop Burroughs, thought Leroy—that was his name—meant to court me.

*I* thought differently because Leroy hadn't spoken to *me* about it. He did make plans with me following that.

Then one evening after his job, and after I got off work, he took me to a restaurant—for a date, a real sit-down dinner.

# *More Growing To Do*

After all these years, I can't tell you how I wound up leaving Mom and Pop Burroughs' home to wind up in an apartment in a building with my personable friend J. Still, I did. J and I had two bedrooms, a kitchen, and a bath. At that little place, I pressed my hair with a hot comb, and I bumped it with my curling irons.

I did J's thick hair, which I made look amazing; every once in a while, I even did the hair of a few others. Leroy, tall and adored, was still around. He was there every now and again, but I wasn't crazy about him. He had a lot going on and many people were pulling at him, demanding his attention.

I can't say I loved my new life, but I did like it, and I was looking to improve it.

In church and at different meetings, I met many people. At one meeting, I met a little man who had been blowing a saxophone. Afterward, it seemed he was running back 'n forth to Gethsemane. He kept coming over to my church to look for me.

Well, when tall red Leroy heard that Sax, a saxophone man, was looking for me, Lee figured he had better get on some time, even though he was seeing another young man's cousin, a female. Tall red thought I didn't know. One night he walked me to my door. Outside the apartment with J, tall red told me he was going to marry me.

I asked, "Don't I have a say?" I also thought, 'What kind of crazy stuff is this?' This was before the Women's Liberation movement, but I further asked, "How do you know *I* want to marry *you*?"

All these years later, I don't even remember Leroy's answer. I guess he'd just made up his mind. I really believe it had something to do with his friend, Oscar…

Upon Leroy introducing me to Oscar, the friend announced I was the marrying kind. That Oscar was a jovial sort. To this day, I do believe he prompted Leroy to really get on his little horse and get after me. Oscar had indeed said I was smart. His perception caused me to wonder if he could see that I wasn't all that interested in his friend by that time. I wanted no playing, no grey areas, and no back 'n forth. I was a serious young woman. I was nearly alone in the world, *and* I wasn't getting younger.

I later found out Leroy really had told Oscar they had to go to Inwood, to my church, because the other man with the saxophone was beating Leroy's time. Weeks later, Leroy gave me a ring.

Was it romantic? Back then, I didn't have that on my mind. We didn't have many lovey-dovey movies either to fuel my imagination. I only know the ring was decent. Still, I wasn't one for a whole lot of fanfare. To me, the engagement was just something that was happening.

Yet I had indeed prayed since I was getting older, I thought. In prayer, I told God that I didn't want to keep winding up alone. As a twenty-something, I asked Him for someone with whom I could go to church, someone that I would not have to fight. My parents' fights were disturbing memories that I didn't want in my own marriage.

This is where I have to tell you... Be careful what you pray for; more importantly, in prayer, *be specific*. I say so because I got just what I asked for. Had I known to ask for more, I would have. Then my Heavenly Father would have granted that, too.

Well, I no longer lived with Mom and Pop Burroughs, but they were my parental figures, so Lee and I approached them with our plans. Although my pastor and his wife weren't happy that their church would lose me, they were delighted overall. The Burroughs understood that I'd have to go to church wherever my husband went.

The daughters of the other pastor in Far Rockaway heard and were a bit upset with me. My other friends felt I'd dropped them. Being young and busy, maybe I had, but I wanted them to know I'd still see them. I wondered if they wanted to hold onto me, although there was no real place for me at their church, not one where I could work with a choir, which was always my heart's desire.

I remember singing *God Don't Want No Coward Soldiers*. I did so at a big gathering. It was a state meeting held at Washington Temple in Brooklyn. Bishop Frederick Douglas —F.D.— Washington, the great orator, was the pastor. On the night that different choirs sang, I sang with Leroy's North Shore District Choir, and I had the energy of the Lord. Although I often had bouts of shyness, and though I repeatedly tried to hide, that night, I could not. There were so many people, including bishops, who stood up and were peering through all those who were standing. Like other audience members, they were trying to glimpse the person singing under the unction of the Holy Spirit…me.

Looking back over my life, I see that the glory of the Lord has always brought me to the front. In *Proverbs 18* verse *16*, the bible says *a person's gift makes room for them and brings them before people of prominence.* So if you are doing something, do it with humbleness of heart. Don't be haughty and do not act ugly. Please don't think you are everything, or that will be your reward. However, if you do the opposite, God will reward you.

# Love Triangle

Confusion was brewing. If you read books 1 &
2 of this series, you know that I had already lived
through enough dramacon—drama and confusion—
to recognize the stirrings. I could sense it, even
before things began to boil over. That was why I
wound up moving from the apartment that I shared
with my female friend, J.

I moved to one in Queens. At least there, at the
new place, owned by an older couple named
Simmons, I would not wind up in consternation. At
least I could be comfortable there, whereas I no
longer felt that way with J, who was no longer so
personable…

Jessica Janna & April Alisa Marquette

I told you, at that time, I was naïve. In looking back, I think perhaps J liked Leroy; he could be ever so charming, and Lee was handsome—but he was courting *me*. I believe J fell for him, or she may have liked him all along. I don't know.

What a triangle! Therefore, all of a sudden, things became uncomfortable. Things were said, and other things happened. It is not my way to spread slander, as you know by now. Therefore, we will leave it at that.

Looking back, though, I sometimes think I should have run, but then I wouldn't have this particular story to tell. Anyway, peering over my shoulder, I could see that there was hurt, and there were also bad feelings.

Therefore, alone, again, at my latest tiny apartment, with my boxes stored in the Simmons' basement, I felt a bit homesick, but then again, maybe I didn't. I really just felt sad once in a while. I missed my family and my church back in Arkansas, and I missed some of the people I had known at home. Often, we miss what is in the rearview mirror when what we are currently experiencing is a bit unfavorable.

I can tell you too that I missed doing hair, at which I was terrific. I missed prettying-up people. Sure, I had my cosmetology license, which was stored away with my other things in the basement, but I wasn't using it. I was now a domestic worker. I even thought about some of the fellows I'd left behind in the Midwest.

I realized nothing had ever materialized with them because of my mother. Ms. Cleo had been very strict, and she'd been protective. Her reasons, we discussed in books 1 and 2. I realized nothing with the guys back home had come to be either because I'd never taken very many people seriously.

Since I was by myself, I returned to prayer a lot of the time. Playtime was over. I had to seek the Holy Spirit. I needed to learn my next move.

Was I going to marry Leroy, or would I move on?

I had to wait and see.

## *Wedding Planner*

We were really doing it! Leroy and I were seeing each other regularly on Saturdays, and we started planning our wedding. I told you he'd given me a ring. It was a diamond in a white gold setting. He had taken me to a Chinese restaurant, but I can't remember whether he gave me the ring in the restaurant or elsewhere.

As we worked on this book, my daughter asked if things were romantic. I don't believe that planning a wedding is; it's time-consuming, first of all. Then it's work. I think I felt dispassionate because I knew that in life, I had to keep moving. I had to keep getting up. I needed to remain employed. I had to keep my prayer life active. That was how life was for me.

It was a different time. As a young woman, I wasn't materialistic. You know how nowadays people might say, "I want this kind of ring, or I just have to have that venue?" Well, back fifty-plus years, those things weren't on my mind. I did think about them years later, but back then, we weren't in as great a materialistic process as people are now. I simply wanted a lovely wedding, after we had started planning it.

This was in the nineteen-sixties, and people, who subsequently came to prominence in ministry, who are now well-known, bishops, evangelists, and the like, happened to be Leroy and my friends. Since they were, I asked the young ladies, and he asked the young men if they would be in our wedding. Then some of the ladies and I went to a bridal shop in Jamaica, New York. My sister-in-law-to-be joined us. I picked the bridesmaid's dress style and color, a mauve/magenta, which they liked. The bridesmaids bought satin pumps. Then the ladies had to have them died to match their dresses. Why on earth are those shoes so very uncomfortable?

Leroy's sister was my maid of honor. I didn't have my sisters because they were in the south and the Midwest. I didn't dwell on that, but thought about the design of my dress. I had it in mind, so I began to make it—by hand. I was employed, but I went to my tiny apartment at night. There, I worked on my dress. You may recall that my mother was a seamstress, from whom I had learned.

My dress was eggshell-colored satin. Fabric wasn't as expensive then as it is now. I put lace-embroidered flowers on the bodice of my dress. I made long fitted sleeves that came to a point on the back of my hand. I sewed a row of pretty little buttons down the sleeve-backs. My dress had a scalloped train and a row of the same pretty buttons that closed it in the rear. The veil I bought.

My Baby Sis, whom you 'met' before, was eighteen or nineteen at the time—if she was that old. She and my mother came to the wedding. Leroy and my nuptials were not held at Mom and Pop Burroughs' church but at a bigger one in St. Albans, New York. Lee and I picked the church on

Baisley Boulevard because of my husband-to-be; he was from a big family, and there would be lots of his people attending. Since he'd lived in New York all of his life, it seemed he knew everyone. At our wedding ceremony, both Leroy's pastor and my pastor officiated, in tandem.

Our reception was held at a large dining hall. Others from churches all over the state had planned it. Their efforts were spearheaded by a woman called Mother Rosie. I don't exactly remember, but I think we had chicken, fish, and roast beef. The wedding cake, purchased by my mother-in-law, was three or four tiers high.

No—to answer my daughter's question—there was no dancing at the reception. I know she was teasing me. She asked while we were working on this, but back then, many church people believed dancing was a sin, so it wasn't even thought of because it wasn't allowed.

I felt like many people attended my wedding and reception for one reason. I felt the same about some of those who'd agreed to serve; I think they did so just to see who their precious Leroy had married.

One older woman even said to me, "You came to New York and got our most-wanted bachelor!"

# Life after Marriage

Lee and I had no honeymoon. We went to a little apartment that he had in a finished basement. We lived there for a while. It wasn't bad at all, and it was in a lovely house.

In the hustle and bustle of getting ready for my wedding and all that followed, I left my boxes in storage at the Simmons' house, back where I'd had my apartment after leaving my friend J.

I kept meaning to get over there and get my things. Lee even said he would go get them for me, but with him being the Minister of Music at his church, neither of us did it. We continued doing things like working, going to church, and adjusting to our new life.

After about six months, we moved to a first-floor apartment in Queens that had a park nearby. By this time, I was pregnant. I was severely ill, but I was yet working— remember Dr. Unger? He'd told me about the Black Jews. I believe I was working for his family at the time, and daily, I rode the bus to work.

My new family, my husband's family, was different from my own in many ways, one of which was: there were a lot of them! They were boisterous when they got together, as large families often are. Everyone, it seemed, spoke and laughed all at the same time. There were numerous aunts, uncles, and cousins. Interaction with them caused me to think about Mother and my little family—that was relatively quiet—back home.

At the time, I was going to the doctor for prenatal visits. To me, it seemed as though no one was excited that I was having a baby. There were already grandchildren in my family, and Leroy's as well. His family had quite a few, so if anyone was excited, I didn't know it.

I'd left Mom and Pop Burroughs' church by this time and had started attending my new husband's church. There, in addition to his music duties, Leroy was also a minister. I noticed that the women liked my husband, a little too much, maybe because he was the music man. I didn't like the way they were hugging him and looking funny at me because I'd married the man they wanted.

I had to tell my husband about all that hugging business. I said some of those the women's intentions weren't pure or innocent—if that was what he wanted to think. I never really thought that maybe he wasn't pure or innocent.

At this new church, they would ask me to sing. Ministering in song, I sang *Were You There; when they crucified my Lord/when they laid Him in the tomb*? Some people told me afterward that they got the shivers whenever I sang that song because I created a picture of Christ on the cross. Others said they could feel the Lord's presence. I also sang the hymns: *Down at the Cross* and *Let us Break Bread Together*. Often I sang the latter for communion.

At different meetings, I sang *God Specializes*, and people cried and gave their lives to the Lord.

Others reported getting healed or set free from various types of addictions or maladies when I allowed the Holy Spirit to use me.

If you're reading this and need healing in any area, just know that by the time you finish this book, God will have begun to transform things in your life. Why? –Simply because His Holy Spirit does that. He flows, in this case, from me to you. He will flow from the words on this page right to your heart.

The Holy Spirit is aware of every one of your needs. I know there are those of you who might think you're too far away, or too far gone—because of what you've done—for the Holy Spirit to care about you. Not true. You are God's child. His Holy Spirit, our comforter, will never forget you. He will not forsake you. *People* might let you down, they may even beat you down, and others may leave you, but the Holy Spirit will not. However, He is a gentleman. I heard someone say that once; the Holy Spirit won't barge into your life. You must invite Him in. Just reach for him; do so in your heart. Ask Him to help you. Ask Him to transform your life, if that's what you need. Whatever you need, He knows, and He will help you with it. He won't do it the way you think, but after what you've asked for is accomplished, thank Him. And let the Holy Spirit keep working in your life, and in *you.*

I can tell you these things because, after eight decades, I know. The Holy Spirit works. I have seen his handiwork, time and again. I know He will meet you at the point of your need.

## *Unwanted News*

One day I received terrible news. This, to me, was the most unwanted news. Back in Chicago, my beloved Cousin was killed. You met her in the book before this one, *Sowing*. She had been my best Cousin, the one with whom I'd gone to live. She had done many things for me, and she had even entrusted me with the care of her children. (I am blowing out breaths of sorrow even now as I speak of it.)

It appears some crazy man who thought he was in love with her couldn't let her go. She wanted to move on from him, but he couldn't see her doing so.

It is awful when people really don't know what love is. Love is not cruel or clutching, and it is not cloying, suffocating, or self-serving. True love only wants happiness for the one that is loved.

Well, from what I learned, this man told Cousin that if he couldn't have her, no one could. We now see he meant that, and we also see that what he called love certainly was not!

I would like it if more people would commit the definition of Love—God's definition—to memory. Then many families would be spared grief, and they would not have to do what Lee and I wound up doing. We attended Cousin's funeral. She had been such a beautiful woman, inside and out, *and* she was the mother of several boys. Those young men had to finish growing up without her.

Those kids were robbed of beautiful occasions like Mother's Day and their mom's birthday!

In the bible *I Corinthians* chapter *13, verses 4 through 7* reads as follows:

*Love is patient*; love *is kind. It does not envy, it does not boast, it is not proud. It is not rude, it is not self-seeking, it is not easily angered, it keeps no record of wrongs. Love does not delight in evil but rejoices with the truth. It always protects, always trusts, always hopes, always perseveres.* NIV

This is love, by God's standards. It is the love that we should strive to practice every day.

As if the news about my Cousin was not enough, I found out about Mrs. Simmons, the woman who owned the house where I'd lived before I got married. She wound up with cancer.

Subsequently, she died. Her home caught afire too, somehow, and burned up. My boxes were still in her basement, and I had never gotten back there to retrieve them. Now you see why it's not good to procrastinate; one of those boxes contained my beauty license.

So many things to feel bad about, I thought. So many others to ponder and wonder why they'd happened. In life, this is often the case. Yet we must remember that we have to let go to reap the good that God has for us. We must relinquish. We shouldn't mentally keep replaying ugly incidents. Things happen; we remember them, but we don't want to nurse the troublesome. I remind myself that I've yet got life. Then I attempt to move forward in Jesus' name.

## *Come Now—Please!*

I was having a baby. I knew because I was continually ill. The morning sickness was terrible. I was irregular too and couldn't really eat. Then when I did consume something, I could hardly digest it. It refused to stay down…so I started eating baby food. Then where I had been tall and slender all my life, that baby food, plus the baby, put weight on me.

I had heartburn for days, too. Aware of this, some people said my baby must have been coming here with a lot of hair. You know those and other sayings are old wives' tales.

While searching for baby names, I liked the name April and Marquette. I wanted to pronounce it Mar-KWET, not Mar-KET. I also liked Elissa, but I liked Alisa better.

My husband had a cousin named Honey. Bless her sweet soul; she was my friend. Before my baby came, precious Honey gave me a beautiful blue coach carriage. Boy was it big and heavy! It had whitewall wheels with shiny metal spokes. It really was like a Cadillac for an infant.

My sister-in-law threw me a baby shower. Those women, and others, didn't have to do things for me but did; they wanted to, and I was grateful.

Then there was no more working for me. When the time arrived for me to have my baby, I was in labor all night. It seemed the infant would not drop down. It went on for so long… My husband had been present, but he had to go to work. He was amid building a business. He had a clothing store uptown in Harlem. In it, he even sold wigs, jewelry, and Afro-Centric items. Sure, Lee had taken me to the hospital. After a while, he even came back. However, for the most part, I was by myself—just me and Jesus, and that baby who was determined to stay in my womb.

I hadn't dilated much while lying on the table for all that long time. I could hear the hospital people discussing what to do with me. I heard them say *if she… baby won't drop down…C-section…* It went on for most of that evening.

I was in agony and wound up going in and out of consciousness. There was a coalition of doctors who were concerned about doing a cesarean section. Back then, that type of operation wasn't performed as much as it is today. Someone even sent for the hospital priest, to administer my last rites!

I wound up having to push so hard that I lost all my wind. Then I simply had to start fighting for my life. I had to get hold of myself in that hospital, through the Holy Spirit. I was sweating and nearly incoherent, but deep within; I knew I had to allow Him to take charge of that situation.

I had to reach past the break—the broken place where fear and torment reside. I had to remember. I had been promised certain things; I knew the Holy Spirit had work for me to do. I could not go out like that; it was too soon in my life. I wanted to live and see the salvation of the Lord.

Therefore, I managed to request my own clergy. I was out of it, so I don't rightly recall whether my preacher—my husband's Pastor—came. I genuinely believe he did. I vaguely remember seeing him.

I was further lapsing into incoherence and sweating profusely. Back then, having babies was a bit different than it is with today's technology. Had I not been fully exhausted and miserable, I'd have told that baby, "*Come now—please!*"

I do know I cried, when I could muster the strength to do so. I was drained. It seemed like it was much later when the hospital Priest appeared.

Then finally, late that evening, my baby decided to come. To aid the arrival, the doctor cut me. I was nearly unaware, being so wiped out, lying on that hard table. After the baby came, the doctor had to sew me up. I was then taken to a different room to get some kind of recovery.

The hospital staff brought the baby to me. I had a little red girl! She had sandy hair, just like her father. I named her *April Alisa Marquette*.

A nurse said, "That sure is a long name to hang on a little girl."

I knew, though, that the name would one day serve her well. Yes, since April means *to open*, and Alisa means *great happiness* in Hebrew. I'd chosen Marquette because Father Jacques Marquette, a French Jesuit missionary, had been an explorer. All of those things, open doors, happiness, and the fearlessness to explore, I wanted for my girl.

My husband appeared at the hospital, as did some of his aunts and my mother-in-law. After that terribly hard labor, I was out of it. All that fighting to give birth dulled my memory, but I knew one thing. *I had become a mother*! –Me, the girl who had been alone for most of her life. I had become a woman. I had now become April's mom.

*God sets the solitary in families…*

I do remember that another woman behind me died. That stuck with me. Thinking about the horror of all I'd been through, I vowed I would never do it again. However, the nurses didn't believe me. They said, "You say that now, but you'll be back." They claimed it always happened again.

When it was time for me to leave the hospital, instead of going back to Lee and my and apartment by the park, I went to my mother-in-law's home. There I slept on a sofa bed. While getting up and down to tend my new baby, I experienced the detrimental. My stitches burst. Then I wound up with a persistent fever. It was a sign that I'd gotten an infection.

My mother-in-law took me to her family practitioner. Now remember, when my baby was born, I had tearing. Therefore, I'd had an episiotomy. That's the medical term for when a doctor stitches a woman up after a complicated birth. Mine happened to be a botched job; I was stitched incorrectly or too quickly, so I wound up at my mother-in-law's physician with terrible bleeding. This new doctor didn't want to touch me.

He told my in-law, "Get her out of here. Take her back to whoever made this mess."

In pain that threatened to double me over, I had to go back to the hospital where I'd delivered my baby. In time, they 'worked at' helping me. Back then, at medical facilities, people who looked like me did not receive the best care. Sadly, today, that is still often the case. It is due to systematic racism and hatred passed down from one generation to the next—when hatred is not God's way.

Afterward, I felt it was time to go back to my home by the park. There, I had pictures taken of my baby. I carried my little one everywhere. I dressed her in the cute things we'd received from many of the saints. I was working on getting myself straight, too, getting rid of that infection, so I sat in tubs of saltwater. All throughout, I was doing what mothers do, feeding, changing, bathing, check-ups, nursing, substituting formula, and putting the baby in her carriage to go buy something for dinner.

Once in a while, on the street, people stopped me for a look at my baby. In church, I yet sang solos when Pastor called on me. I wasn't really heavy now since I'd quit the baby food diet a good while before I'd delivered. I was on the mend, and I was learning to love in a way that I had never before known. I was learning to love my child as our Heavenly Father loves us, His children, without reserve.

## *Shaken Up*

Fourteen months later, just as the nurses had predicted, I was expecting, again. This time, pregnant with my second child, I was threatening a miscarriage. Therefore, I was placed on bed rest. I had to take medication, too, pills that I put under my tongue. I'd lie down like I'd been instructed, but I had to get up to take care of my first baby. Lee, my husband, would come home at different times to help, but I wouldn't—I just could not  stay in bed.

And would you believe…with all that, we moved!

With this pregnancy, women I knew were fascinated with the maternity outfits that I found time to make. Many church people were also charmed by my April. What a little character she was.

Some mothers do everything for baby and forget themselves. I did not. I'd always fix myself up nice, too. People remarked on how pretty I looked in the clothes I created. If you remember, I'd done so since I had been young; it was one of my passions.

One day I fell. At the time, I was visibly pregnant with my second child, and I had my first daughter in my arms. I even had a heavy bag of necessities slung over my shoulder. I was running—I had to—if I was going to catch my bus. As I was doing so, I *hit the ground.*

I landed on my protruding *belly*! My first baby bounced out of my arms. She wound up seated on the ground, looking at me. Thank God she wasn't hurt, nor did she cry, but I am sure that, like my unborn baby and me, my girl was a bit shaken up.

With the help of others, I managed to rise and get moving. My midsection hurt, and my knees were sore, but those things were minor. They went away. Still, I've never forgotten that shake-up.

Since I often had to go to the doctor for prenatal visits, I wound up taking a cab one day. And wouldn't you know? On this day, the driver got us into an accident! Him, me, my first baby, and my unborn child. My poor second baby, boy, were they getting shaken up, right along with my April and me.

# A Mother, Again

Labor with my second baby wasn't as hard as with my first. Then when this baby was born, she looked so different from her sister. She wasn't red.

As an adult, my second daughter will often glance at her baby picture. She claims she looked like a little old man. I tell her to stop talking about my baby. My baby was beautiful and just perfect.

I named my first girl, but I allowed my older sister to name my second. With the girls, I had no sibling issues. My big girl was often simply trying to figure out our second baby, Melody Lila. April would look at her sister's tiny hands. She'd look all over the baby like she was fascinated.

April was always an old witchy girl; by that, I mean when she came here, in a lot of ways, she already seemed like an adult. She was just in a tiny body. Some children are like that. It was why I was worried that she wouldn't really want the new baby to be there. Therefore, I put my first girl in the equation so she wouldn't feel left out. This way, she could deal with the baby.

Now my first girl never crawled. One day she just decided to stand. Using a chair, she pulled her tiny self up and took her first steps. However, as her sister grew, April had somebody to play with. So she wound up crawling to play with her baby sister, who had such a sweet personality. As she grew, my new baby, Melody Lila, got in the mode of playing with things and handing them to her big sister.

With two babies, for me, motherhood became real work. But I put both girls in the coach carriage, and we were off, especially when my big baby decided she no longer wanted to walk. Melody Lila, my second girl, whom we call Diamond, did not do a lot of crying. When she did, she had stomach troubles, but she was not a hollering baby.

During this time, our Pastor took sick. Although my husband was building his business, he also spent time becoming an elder in the church. Lee had been in training and the season came when he went before the board. Then one bishop told him there were things on which he was being slack. This bishop offered my husband, a young man, constructive criticism.

Back on the home front, our Pastor wound up in the hospital. However, when he came out, he set the church in order. Our Pastor made my husband his first assistant. He made an older West Indian man the second assistant. Lee's cousin was the third. Looking back, I now believe Pastor was preparing all of us for the inevitable.

I was with child again, and my little family moved, this time to a lovely place in Brooklyn. I often found myself praying for a son. Yet, when I visited the doctor's office, I did not want to be told the sex of my baby. I simply asked God to allow me to know how to raise both the boy and the girl. That experience I wanted.

When my third baby came, the occurrence was entirely different from the prior two. My *boy* was in a hurry to get here. There was no trauma, and he was the most straightforward delivery.

Before the hospital workers could get me fully on the table, my boy was putting in an appearance.

Hospitals kept new mothers a requisite three days back then, so I stayed. It was on a Sunday that I went home. Entering the house, I just knew… something was *wrong*. I could feel it, although at the moment I did not know what it was.

## *An Ordeal*

A lovely sister from Gethsemane, my old church, had been watching my small girls. This lady had agreed to do so before I'd gone to the hospital to deliver my son.

Now that I was home, the moment I entered the house, I knew something was amiss. It was the discernment of the Holy Spirit. Gently, He will warn us of things to come. I felt sick, but it wasn't sickness for *me*. I was murmuring to myself that something was not right—not that I thought the sister had done anything untoward. However, a mother's intuition will also kick in at certain times. Then she needs to pay attention.

I went into my children's room, and my second girl was lying down, facing away from me. Very attached to me, she had not toddled to greet me; that was not a good sign. When I could see her little face, her eyes were rolling up into her head. Then my baby girl started regurgitating. She also had diarrhea. Tending her, I got to cleaning and mopping. Settling my new infant boy, too, that first afternoon out of the hospital, I also answered my big girl's questions.

As I resumed my motherly duties, I noticed that my toddler girl kept falling down on her little head because she was too weak to get up. Since it was Sunday, my husband was at church. I was handling things, but I really was becoming scared. There I was, tending a newborn, my eldest, and my ailing middle child—whose sickness went on, over into the night. I did the best I could do for her.

Early in the morning, however, I was up. Knowing my toddler girl wasn't getting better; I told my husband that I was taking Melody Lila to the hospital. Mind you now, he had already taken her to see a doctor. He'd done so the day before, after he'd come in from church, where he was now assuming some of our ailing pastor's duties. The medical staff had given my little girl sugar-water and had sent her and my husband home; negligence is what I'm now thinking. Nonetheless, that next morning, I was adamant. I told Lee, "My child is dying." I knew it in my heart.

So I took her to the hospital. When I got there, the staff was messing around. They were quite unconcerned. My baby girl was so weak that her eyes were walling back in her head. So you know I prayed. Again, like I'd had to do when I was giving birth to April, I took a stand. I had to get hold of myself. Within, I had to reach down, past the break—that awful nagging fear which said I would lose my precious girl. I had to remember whose I am, and in whom I believe. I had to allow the Holy Spirit to take charge of that situation. It was not easy; I was shaking. Fear not only makes the hands tremble, but it makes the mind quake.

I'll tell you, though…somewhere inside a believer, when they are in the midst of turmoil, the knowledge of what they've been through and how they came through begins to germinate. Past experiences of deliverance come to mind. That's what happened to me. Then inside, although I wasn't fully conscious of it, I recalled that I had come through many things. The Holy Spirit had been there. I'd climbed proverbial hills and up the rough side of the mountain. Through all of it, the Holy Spirit had been my source, and my protection.

*Psalms 91* verse *11* says: *For He shall give His angels charge over thee, to keep thee in all thy ways.* So deep down, past the fear that my girl was slipping away, I knew my Redeemer would meet me, there, in that hospital, at the point of my need.

I remembered that *Psalms 91* also says, in verse *16*: *With long life will I satisfy, and show him* [or her] *my salvation.* So I yielded to the promises in the word. *I was not going to lose my child*! Looking back, I realize it was only then that I released my faith. As believers, *we have authority!* In Luke 10:9, Jesus said, *"Behold, I give unto you power..."* So in faith, I walked up to that desk. In the power of the Holy Spirit I went because *this time*, I told myself, *someone* was *going to* hear me. Someone was *going to* help me.

I carried my precious girl to the front, at the same time that the Holy Spirit prompted the head nurse to come down to the desk. She saw my limp baby in my arms. She saw me literally pleading, asking for help, right then. The head nurse pulled at the skin on my baby's face. Seeing that there was no resilience, she said, "This baby's dehydrated..." That woman got everyone to hopping. She started calling out all kinds of orders.

You can't tell me the Holy Spirit won't show up. I've seen Him do it many times.

Then upstairs, there were mean nurses, probably overworked, over-tired, under-valued, and underpaid, but mean just the same. Through the hospital grapevine, they might have heard about my little girl and me. They may have felt as though I had gotten their counterparts downstairs in some type of trouble. Whatever the case, they spoke to me in wicked voices, like I was being paranoid, or like my baby's case was no different and no more critical or severe than anyone else's.

They were condescending and nasty when they stated, "Miss, go out." They spoke of my baby, "She is not going to die."

I did not trust them. *Nevertheless*, I did—and I do—trust the Holy Spirit! I have to tell you, my heart was breaking then because my baby girl was crying. She saw me leaving. I was being put out. Still, my baby could not have known that I was being shoved out of the ward. I hate to remember it, the way she was in that railed iron bed, trying to get up. She was so weak; she was falling down, but reaching for me, and sobbing. All these years later, I can still remember. Then those devils, them ratchet nurses, had the nerve to tie the baby sheet around my little one's legs. They claimed they did it so she couldn't climb out of bed! Sometimes, I know people let the devil use them. They pay for it too.

At that moment, I could only ask the Lord to watch over my baby.

When I saw my beautiful girl again, her little nose ran, and she was tied like some animal. It broke my heart. I tried to shush her as I noticed she was being fed intravenously. I tried to comfort her. Although I hated to, after a while I had to leave her again because I had two other babies at home, and my husband couldn't sit with them all day. He had to work to provide for us, his family.

My baby girl wound up having to stay at that hospital for over a week. My time away from the hospital was spent fervently praying, while I tended my infant boy and my eldest. Inside, I felt sick with worry, but I had to keep giving it to the Lord.

I had no other family present, so I asked my in-laws to go up to the hospital. I just wanted someone to be with my Melody Lila. I wanted those nasty nurses to know they couldn't get away with doing just anything to her. I felt like my in-laws took their time about going, but then again, I have to remember. What is important to one person may not be as important to another. So I prayed some more.

My older sister—whom you met in Book 1 of this series—was a teacher by this time. She was in New York, visiting. My beloved pastor and his sweet wife from Arkansas came too; what a blessing! I was thrilled. My mother traveled, and it was something she did not often do. She appeared at my home and was a major Godsend. I was so glad to see her because I'd previously felt I was floating out of myself. I had experienced so much in such a short time. I truly felt nauseous—like I was on a runaway train. Still, the Holy Spirit had sent aid.

Mother cared for my oldest girl and my baby boy; thus, allowing me to be up at that hospital. Believing she would lessen my load, one day Mother even said, "I can help you, Jessie..." Then she made me an offer. "When I go home, I'll take big girl back with me."

I had to say no. Mind you now, I wasn't being ungrateful. "You raised your children," I told Mother. I felt it would have been unfair for me to push my child off on my mom, although Lord knew, at the time, I could have used her help. However, I did not want my oldest daughter away or to wind up not knowing me. That is what would have happened had she been reared in Arkansas with her grandmother while I was in New York.

Suffice it to say, the Holy Spirit brought my Melody Lila through, safe and sound! I am rejoicing.

You know, old people often love hymns, and through that experience and others, I have learned why. Those songs, borne of the human experience, touch the soul and say what we sometimes cannot say. Hymns depict turmoil –but also how the Holy Spirit will bring us through. I believe that's why I have always loved the hymn *I Must Tell Jesus*. I love the phrase: *He ever loves and cares for His own.*

I also love to sing the part of *Amazing Grace* that says, *'Tis grace hath brought me safe thus far, and grace will lead me home.*

Hallelujah. Our God be praised.

## *The Boy...*

My sweet boy wasn't a howling baby. He had a pleasant disposition. He was just so happy to be there in our little family. I'd named him after his father, but I had not named him Leroy [Lee-Roy]. I'd named him LeRoy—meaning the royal one, which he has grown up believing. His middle name was a combination of those of his paternal grandparents.

Motherhood was work now, with my new baby boy, plus two girls, but I got things done. I also found out that my second girl had contracted something vicious, an intestinal virus. It had nearly killed her. After speaking with the sister who'd kept her, I made a deduction. My toddler had a pacifier on a string around her neck. That was what we did in those days. Then in the Laundromat, she'd been crawling on the floor. So, of course, her pacifier had most likely been on the floor, too. I did not blame the sister who had so graciously kept my girls for me. That lady did my laundry and managed my household while I'd been in the hospital. The very same thing could have happened had my toddler been with me. I simply tried not to ponder how things could have quickly gone the other way, had not the Holy Spirit intervened, and had He not caused my toddler to receive the right medical care.

Forgetting those things, for me, each day seemed busier than the one before. Still, I got all my babies' little clothes washed. I ironed, I took my husband's shirts to the cleaners to be starched, and I cooked dinner. I managed to keep the bigger kids clean and supervised while I fed the baby boy. I got doctor visits and shots out of the way. I grocery shopped, and mopped, and whatever else. Company sometimes came for a bit, from my old church, or from my husband's church. Then it was back to washing and combing hair. During bath time, I got splashed and soaked. I gave medicine, and was bone-tired. I read stories, over and over again, mostly the one about the mama bear.

I ignored wheedling. I said, "No whining." I got giggles after tickling. I called out, more times than I remember, "It's bedtime." I chuckled at silly stuff. I changed bedding. I really wanted conversations with adults, just so I could stay sane. I wiped noses and behinds. I needed only a few hours to myself, but then again, as a new mother, I would have been too worried to enjoy the respite.

As Mommy, I ate what the kids would not— bread crusts, peanut butter, soggy cereal, drying fruit, and baloney. I drank warm milk just because I couldn't bear to see it wasted. I gained weight. I often heard the 'Sesame Street' song playing, even in my head. I picked up toys and began teaching the girls songs—hymns, first and foremost. I sang Nat King Cole, Big Band ballads and Negro Spirituals to all my babies. We said prayers. I taught ABCs, manners, and colors. We kept little things out of small ears, noses, and mouths—I needed no more trips to the emergency room. I let the girls hold their brother, who was growing and happy. I said, "No pinching." I hunted the girls down when they got quiet. I knew that busy oldest one might have been in their room, gladly teaching her sister to use crayons on a wall. I hugged and potty-trained. I said, "Put your things in the toy box before Daddy gets home." I didn't want him falling over kid stuff.

I got them, and myself, dressed. We went to church, not only on Sundays, but to revivals in the evenings. My husband went to work. When he was at home, he helped out and marveled at the kids' growth and at things they said. Where did they come up with that stuff? They giggled and basked in the glow of his presence. He was tickled. They adored him—while I was relegated to role of disciplinarian.

We often took all three babies and trekked up to Harlem to work together in the growing business. I got kisses and only a few hours of sleep, and it was not nearly enough!

Before we'd gotten married, I hadn't known it would seem like every day there would be more and more for both me and my husband to do.

Away from home, I didn't know all the details of our Pastor's illness, but I believe he had a stroke. I could be wrong, and it could have been a heart attack. I do know that afterward, he couldn't talk that well. Yet he asked us to bring 'the boy.' That was what he called my third baby. The Pastor said he wanted to see my husband's son.

For our Pastor, my husband was like a son. Thus, it only made sense that Pastor wanted to see

Lee's son. Obliging, we trekked from Brooklyn to the home of our shepherd. Pastor was happy to see our baby. He kept saying, "The boy…the boy…"

Pastor managed to tell my husband, "You'll have to do some going to keep up with that young woman." Although he'd spoken of ministry, at the time, neither of us knew exactly what he meant.

Then…our Pastor died. He left us; as parishioners, we were bewildered. It seemed as though it had happened too suddenly. That was an anxiety-filled time. Many church members were devastated, including my in-laws. My husband was, too. His eyes were bloodshot. He existed in a state near to shock because our Pastor had been a second father to him. To our congregation and others, Pastor had been larger than life, almost.

As a young man, Lee admitted to me that he didn't know anything about leading the church; he'd thought Pastor would be there forever—or at least for a good while longer. I felt saddened, for all of us. This wasn't how things were supposed to go. Was it? No flock needs to lose a shepherd.

I had to forget inquiries. My young husband had to do the same. We simply had to find ourselves in a state of yielding. We were slated to be the leaders of our flock. It appeared my husband would likely wind up the Pastor of the Church we attended. God had allowed this to be, so despite feeling frightened, we knew we had to soldier on.

Pastor's funeral was held, not at our church, but at the very same church, the one on Baisley Boulevard where we'd gotten married. Many, many people, dignitaries, and ordinary everyday people attended. For Lee and me, it was both sad and scary.

Back at our church, Pastor's wife and the district missionary had some say in who would be next in line to lead. They let our bishop know that they thought my husband was a good fit, for whatever reasons. I heard that it was said, Leroy fit well, in part, because his wife would not hinder him. I did not hear the exact words, but I was told that was the gist.

After some time, my husband was installed to lead the work. The bishop came out, and at our church all was set in order.

# *Truly Yielding*

Many things happened to me, my husband, and our family in such a short period of time. Sure, I often felt overwhelmed, but I was learning to yield.

That word means to surrender or submit, which I did. I yielded to becoming a young married, and I was learning to live with a husband. Often, I had to submit. Young women occasionally find this concept unimaginable, but understand and receive what I am saying.

Back then, I could argue. I was pretty good at it, and I had a mean streak. I'm not perfect. I thought I needed to have the last word. Yet I had to learn that those actions were not the way to have peace in my home. I am reminded of a question I once heard; *do you want to be right, or do you want to be married?*

In yielding or submitting, in marriage, both partners will often have to put the needs of the other before their own. This creates symmetry, harmony, and a shared bond. It creates a safe space. However, I will admit, it is not the easiest thing to do, especially not without the help of the Holy Spirit. Sometimes we may just want our own way or to defend our personal point of view. At times, that must be put aside.

During the period of which I am speaking, I was learning the complexities of marriage and those of getting along with a new family—my husband's. I was also finding my place in a new church family. I had to further yield to the knowledge that my life, and my married life, would not mirror anyone else's. Our journey was uniquely our own.

My husband and I had a business in Harlem. It was almost as new as our union. So that took time, patience, and planning. Then we needed perseverance on the home front. We had three little *people* who needed lots of time, instruction, and attention.

At that point, my husband and I—young and newly married—were also living in a period of great upheaval and change. It was the nineteen-sixties, and we were heading into the seventies. In America, it was the height of the Civil Rights movement. I had to realize that times were changing. For me, as a young black woman, an

African-American, who had experienced evil Jim Crow segregation firsthand, from my earliest years, the future felt uncertain. Still, I was a mother and a wife. Trying to make my way in the world, I wanted to teach my babies to navigate and not fear the changes that were inevitably arriving.

That period was when Dr. King, Malcolm X, Dr. Betty Shabazz, Medgar Evers, and many others—many of whom my husband and I got to meet—came into prominence. Harlem was abuzz then, and we knew hordes of people. It was a time of tears, upheaval, and bloodshed. We lost many of our Black Princes, the true voices that called for freedom from oppression, racial equality, and change. Yet it was a historic time too, one of triumph and promise, sometimes.

As if those things were not enough, my new husband and I were thrust into ministry. On top of everything, we became pastors, seemingly overnight. Now we were accountable for the souls of others, people who were not our small children. Not only were we pastoring the young, and many times, the un-churched, we were the shepherds for the aged, as well.

What could we teach our elders? I wondered as many of them depended on us. My husband went to see about them, and he held their hands as they left this life. We went to hospitals and jails. We went to graduations, and presided over weddings and funerals. My husband, who was now my pastor, christened babies. I cooked and housed people. I led worship services. I wondered a lot, and prayed.

I often felt God had rolled both Lee and me into a ball and threw us out there. Yet I found myself wanting to do God's will. Thus I yielded. I found the time to pick up my songwriting again. I took it more seriously now, and I wrote with a purpose that I hadn't had, previously. I scribbled and jotted notes and scriptures on any available surface. I voraciously devoured the word as it left the lips and the pens of Kenneth E. Hagin, Oral Roberts, Bishop F. D. Washington, and others of that ilk.

Prayer was a constant in my life. Throughout my busy days, I yielded time for communion with the Holy Spirit. I submitted because I knew one thing. I could not make the journey before me without Him, and not without His guidance.

In yielding, I began a dedicated journey that would teach me about the total person, the triune self. I started a quest to find out what makes human beings whole, in mind, body, and spirit.

I chuckle as I write this because all those years ago, I began this odyssey, and still, I find myself on the same quest, albeit renewed. I am amused, too, because as an adult, my April takes bits of my life and weaves it into her many works of fiction. It is amazing to see and hear about my life through my daughter's eyes.

To me, it is incredible to hear how my Diamond and my Cal, her brother, have mastered the gift of song. Musicians, too, both claim they've followed my footsteps, and I can only give glory to God.

All these years later, I still long to be in the presence of the Holy Spirit; I yet want to be more of what He wants me to be; I ask Him to show me a more excellent way. Now I'm an old woman. Still, I pray and seek the Lord's face. I do so because through many terrible and many lovely things The Holy Spirit has both guided and sustained me.

At the time of this writing, I am in my eighties, and *I am yet yielding*, I am still submitting *to the divine*. I will do so until the day I leave here. Why? –Because the Holy Spirit has been my all.

Won't you let Him be the same to you? I ask because I know one thing; had I not, my journey would not have been as amazing. And it's still getting better! There is more that the Holy Spirit has in store for me. I know it, and I love it.

# *My Thoughts*

*My dear reader, I know I've said it before, but I will repeat it. Amid every occurrence in my life, I have held tightly to my faith and to the Holy Spirit who has carried me.*

*Sure, I've had to cry, and sometimes I've wanted hurtful things to be different, but I have learned to be grateful. It's all been a learning experience. Indeed, I am still learning—to yield.*

*I have accepted that this is my life, the one that I was given. And with this life, I choose to do what I said in previous books: I give it away; that is the best thing that I can do with my life. I give you what I have received, what I've learned. I tell you my story so that perhaps after reviewing my journey, you may be as blessed or more so than I have been.*

*Simply yield, just submit, to the Holy Spirit. He will carry you. He will take you past every ill. I'm not saying things won't happen in your life. However, the Holy Spirit will enable you to forgive—to relinquish—any bad feelings so that you may reap and rejoice!*

*I love you, and daily, I pray for you. It doesn't matter that I might not know your name. You are among the number—you are one of God's own. For you, I request blessings, and I ask that He shower you with wisdom. In this life, wisdom is so necessary. I also ask that the precious Holy Spirit be revealed to you in many unique ways, some of them still, soft and quiet. Then may He be there amid your loud, joyous, and colorful celebrations.*

*Remember, like the palm tree in a storm, you may bend and bow, but you do not have to break.*

*Yield, my dear, and be blessed.*

*Prayerfully,*

*Mama Jess*

# *Acknowledgements*
**Hymns**

*Amazing Grace* - John Newton, pub. 1779

*Down at the Cross* - Elisha A. Hoffman, 1878.
Public Domain

*His Eye is on the Sparrow* - Text: Civilla D. Martin,
Charles H. Gabriel c. 1926.

*I Must Tell Jesus* - Elisha A. Hoffman, 1893 *v. 4 arr.*
Public Domain

*In Times Like These* - Text: Ruth Caye Jones, c. 1972.

*Let us Break Bread Together* – Traditional / Afro-
American Spiritual;
Adapted & arr.  William Farley Smith 1986

## *Thanks*

I thank my daughter, *April Alisa Marquette*, for being wise and curious. These things have allowed her to aid me in bringing my memories to life, again —after eighty—some years. I thank her, too, for trying to Mother me. I know she'll never stop.

I thank my *Diamond*, Melody Lila, for being there—for so many things. With her patient, gentle ways, she is now often my hands and feet. The Healing of the Lord truly resides within this lovely-voiced worship leader.

I thank my son LeRoy, Mr. *Cal* Burns, for being protective. I am amazed at his talent. I am also grateful for his strength, wisdom, and many things, including his simply being…mine.

I thank *God* for these people who came into my life and did not leave. They were once my babies. I am so grateful that they have taken this journey with me. I also thank them because, even after all we've been through, our tremendous ups and downs, these three have become… my very best *friends.*

*I am no longer alone.*

*Mom*

*F*or another glimpse into her life, look for:

# *Chrysalis*
The 'Making' Years

*Jessica Janna*
&
*April Alisa Marquette*

## Non-Fiction

As a wife, a mother, and a business owner in ministry, Jessica finds her life far busier than she ever expected. In this, the chronicling of her 'making' years, she is experiencing the things that will make her...*if* she doesn't allow them to break her.

This account in her inspirational true-life series is jubilant!

*Chrysalis,* is the **fourth** account in
Jessica Janna's optimistic ***Relinquish & Reap*** Series.